# An Adam® Collection by Brian Basset

**Andrews McMeel
Publishing**

Kansas City

**Adam**® may be viewed on the Internet at:
www.uexpress.com

**This book is dedicated
to those who work alone,
who so courageously persevere
over the distractions of home.**

**Other Books by Brian Basset**

Adam

Life in the Fast-Food Lane

Life Begins at 6:40

Minivanity

WHY DON'T YOU AND NICK COME INTO TOWN TODAY AND MEET ME FOR LUNCH? SAY AROUND NOON?

THAT LATE?

THAT'S NORMALLY WHEN PEOPLE EAT LUNCH, ADAM.

NOT WHEN ONE WORKS OUT OF HIS HOME. I USUALLY TAKE LUNCH AROUND 10.

ANY CHANCE YOU COULD DO IT CLOSER TO 1? THAT'S ABOUT WHEN I HAVE DINNER.

OH, REALLY? WHAT DO YOU CALL IT WHEN WE SIT DOWN TO EAT AS A FAMILY EVERY NIGHT?

YOU MEAN MY MIDNIGHT SNACK?

BRIAN BASSET

LAURA, DID YOU SEE THE MESSAGE THEY PUT IN THE SYSTEM?... STAFF RETREAT NEXT SATURDAY. ARE YOU GOING?

Y'KNOW, I CAN'T THINK OF ANYTHING I'D RATHER BE DOING ON MY DAY OFF.

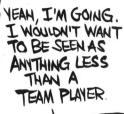

YEAH, I'M GOING. I WOULDN'T WANT TO BE SEEN AS ANYTHING LESS THAN A TEAM PLAYER.

BRIAN BASSET

IT MAY BE TOO LATE FOR THAT.

YOU'RE BARELY SEEN NOW THROUGH ALL THE "DILBERT" CARTOONS THAT YOU'VE TAPED TO YOUR WINDOW.

HEY! GREAT HAIRCUT!

YOU DON'T THINK IT'S TOO SHORT?

NOT AT ALL!

REALLY?? 'CAUSE I THINK HE TOOK TOO MUCH OFF.

BRIAN BASSET

YOU'RE RIGHT. HE TOOK TOO MUCH OFF!

OKAY, OKAY. MAYBE IT HAS BEEN A WHILE SINCE WE LAST FOOLED AROUND.

WHATEVER YOU SAY. I WOULDN'T WANT TO TICK YOU OFF.

UM, JUST A SECOND, UM... SHOULD I BE TIPPING YOU — Y'KNOW, LIKE I DO THE PIZZA DELIVERY GUY?

DEFINITELY **NOT**.

THANKS. ALL THIS TIME I DIDN'T KNOW WHAT THE PROTOCOL WAS.

... THE PIZZA DELIVERY GUY SAID YOU'RE A LOUSY TIPPER.

ADAM, LOOK AT YOUR HOME OFFICE. CORDS *EVERYWHERE!* A LINE FOR YOUR COMPUTER, A LINE FOR YOUR FAX MACHINE. A LINE FOR YOUR PHONE. YOU NEED TO CALL THE **SMALL BUSINESS EXPERTS**.

SANTA'S ELVES?

NOOOO.

THE PEOPLE WHO MAKE MICROMACHINES®??

I WAS THINKING OF THE PHONE COMPANY.

THIS IS THE PHONE COMPANY. HOW MAY WE HELP YOU?

I'D, UH, LIKE TO SPEAK TO SOMEONE IN YOUR HOME-OFFICE DIVISION. I NEED HELP WITH MY HOME OFFICE.

IT'LL BE A FEW MINUTES, SIR. ALL OUR HOME-OFFICE CONSULTANTS ARE EITHER CHANGING DIAPERS, E-MAILING THEIR PALS, OR WATCHING TV.

DID I COME TO THE RIGHT PEOPLE OR WHAT?!!

HI, THIS IS BRAD WITH THE PHONE COMPANY'S HOME-OFFICE DIVISION. THANKS FOR HOLDING. HOW MAY I BE OF SERVICE?

I, UM, WORK OUT OF MY HOUSE AND...

SAY NO MORE—YOU'VE COME TO THE RIGHT SPOT. WE ARE, AFTER ALL, THE SMALL BUSINESS EXPERTS!

SMALL?? YOU'RE A MULTIBILLION-DOLLAR-A-YEAR CONGLOMERATE. WHAT DO YOU KNOW ABOUT "SMALL"??

BRIAN BASSET

ALEXANDER GRAHAM BELL STARTED OUT WITH ONLY ONE PHONE, OKAY!

ENOUGH SAID.

I RUN A SMALL BUSINESS OUT OF MY HOME, AND I, UM, WAS WONDERING HOW YOU, I MEAN THE PHONE COMPANY, CAN HELP ME BE MORE PRODUCTIVE?

WELL... PROVIDING FIRST-RATE SERVICE IN TODAY'S HIGH-TECH WORLD DOESN'T MEAN ABANDONING THE "PERSONAL" TOUCH.

TWANG!

EVERYONE CAN START BY IMPROVING HIS PHONE ETIQUETTE.

BRIAN BASSET

MY PHONE ETIQUETTE IS FINE, THANK YOU VERY MUCH!

SLAM!

NOT THIS SECOND, NICK. I'M ON THE PHONE WITH MY VERY OWN HOME OFFICE CONSULTANT FROM THE PHONE COMPANY.

AS I WAS SAYING, YOUR VOICE IS IMPORTANT—IT HELPS THE LISTENER FORM A MENTAL PICTURE OF YOU. THIS IS KEY WHEN WORKING FROM HOME. YOUR VOICE SHOULD REFLECT SINCERITY, INTEREST AND CONFIDENCE.

BRIAN BASSET

I DO A REALLY GOOD ELMER J. FUDD IMPERSONATION IN THE MORNING WHEN MY VOICE IS STILL ROUGH AND SCRATCHY.

I SUGGEST YOU DON'T ANSWER THE PHONE BEFORE 10 THEN.

THE SELLING OF YOUR COMPANY'S IMAGE TAKES PLACE EVERY TIME YOU USE OR ANSWER THE PHONE. THE WAY EVERY CALL IS HANDLED DETERMINES WHETHER YOU CREATE BUSINESS OR LOSE IT.

BRIAN BASSET

BE HONEST. IF SOMEONE CALLS AND IT'S A BAD TIME TO TALK, POLITELY TELL HIM SO.

DADDY! CLAYTON'S PUTTING MARBLES UP HIS NOSE TO SHOOT AT ME!!

READY... AIM...

ASK THE CALLER WHEN A GOOD TIME WOULD BE TO CALL BACK, MAKING SURE TO NOTE THE CALLER'S NAME, NUMBER, FIRM OR DEPARTMENT.

? I DIDN'T MEAN TO HIT YOU, DAD, HONEST!

HERE ARE A NUMBER OF BASIC TELEPHONE TECHNIQUES NEEDED TO HANDLE CUSTOMERS AND BUSINESS SITUATIONS PROFESSIONALLY — ESPECIALLY WHEN WORKING FROM HOME.

BRIAN BASSET

BE CONSIDERATE. BEWARE OF BACKGROUND NOISES, AND TRY NOT TO CARRY ON TWO CONVERSATIONS AT ONCE... OR THREE.... OR FOUR....

HELPFUL HOME OFFICE PHONE TIPS

TRY TO CONCENTRATE AND SHUT OUT DISTRACTIONS. AVOID DOING OTHER THINGS WHEN CONDUCTING BUSINESS ON THE PHONE.

WHAT AN IDIOT!! HE SHOULD'VE BOUGHT A VOWEL!

BRIAN BASSET

**When working from home, it is critical
to stake out your territory.**

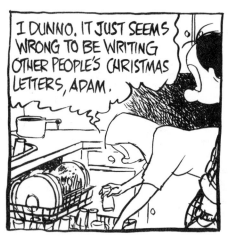

SEASONS GREETINGS FROM HAROLD AND THELMA. WE HOPE THIS FINDS YOU ALL WELL AND HAPPY.

CLICK CLICK CLICK CLICK

IN MARCH, HAROLD HAD KNEE-REPLACEMENT SURGERY. IN JUNE HE WAS FITTED FOR DENTURES.

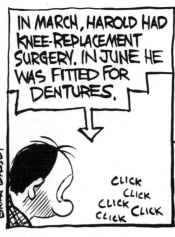

CLICK CLICK CLICK CLICK CLICK

THE HAIR TRANSPLANT HE RECEIVED IN SEPTEMBER IS COMING IN NICELY, AND JUST A FEW WEEKS AGO HE WENT BACK IN TO HAVE HIS LEFT HIP REPLACED.

CLICK CLICK CLICK CLICK

(SIGH) HE'S NOT THE SAME MAN I MARRIED.

CLICK CLICK CLICK CLICK CLICK CLICK

---

WARMEST HOLIDAY WISHES FROM THE **HARRINGTON** HOUSEHOLD. AFTER GETTING DOWNSIZED IN JULY, **TOM** IS BACK ON HIS FEET, BUT AT HALF HIS OLD SALARY WITH NO BENEFITS.

CLICK CLICK CLICK CLICK

**ROB** LETTERED IN SWIMMING AND SOCCER, AND CONTINUES TO MAINTAIN A 4.0 GPA. **PATTI** IS OUR BUDDING GYMNAST, AND SCORED THREE OVERALL FIRST PLACES THIS YEAR!

CLICK CLICK

**JANET** IS A BUSY MOM WITH NO TIME FOR HERSELF WHO CONTINUALLY GIVES AND GIVES AND GIVES.

CLICK CLICK

*THAT'S* GIVES GIVES GIVES GIVES GIVES GIVES.

CLICK CLICK CLICK CLICK

CONSEQUENTLY, DON'T EXPECT ANY PRESENTS FROM HER THIS YEAR.

CLICK CK CLICK CLICK CLICK CLICK

---

ADAM, DID YOU RECEIVE MY FAX LISTING WHAT OUR FAMILY DID THIS PAST YEAR?

YUP. I'M LOOKING AT IT AS WE SPEAK, DAVE.

GOOD. UM, LISTEN... IF POSSIBLE, COULD YOU, Y'KNOW, PUT A POSITIVE SPIN ON THINGS?.. DAVID JR.'S 6-MONTH SENTENCE TO JUVENILE DETENTION NEARLY BROKE HIS MOTHER'S HEART.

POSITIVE SPIN. YOU GOT IT!

...FROM APRIL THROUGH SEPTEMBER, JOY AND LAUGHTER COULD ONCE AGAIN BE HEARD THROUGHOUT THE NEIGHBORHOOD.

CLICK CLICK CLICK CLICK CLICK

ADAM BY BRIAN BASSET

Y'KNOW, ADAM. KATY AND CLAYTON DON'T QUITE SHARE YOUR ENTHUSIASM FOR THE END OF THEIR SUMMER VACATION.

YOU MIGHT TRYING BEING A LITTLE LESS OBVIOUS IN YOUR SMUGNESS.

BRIAN BASSET

WHATEVER DO YOU MEAN?

I'D CALL "HIGH-FIVING" THE CASHIER RINGING UP THE KIDS' BACK TO SCHOOL PURCHASES A BIT MUCH.

HEY. IT WAS A BOOST TO THE ECONOMY! I JUST BEAT HIM TO IT.

PSSST! KATY. ARE YOU AWAKE?

TAP TAP

BRIAN BASSET

YEAH. I CAN'T SLEEP. I'M NERVOUS ABOUT THE FIRST DAY OF SCHOOL.

SAME HERE. I'M AFRAID I'LL GET STUCK SITTING BY SOME KID WHO EATS PASTE.

BUT YOU EAT PASTE.

I KNOW. THAT MEANS LESS FOR ME.

BUS DRIVER, BUS DRIVER, STOP THE BUS!! I THINK WE LEFT SOME CHILDREN AT THE BUS STOP!!!

EMERGENCY EXIT

NOPE. MY MISTAKE.

BRIAN BASSET

IT'S ONLY PARENTS.

**Panel 1:** DAD! QUICK!! HAND ME MY WATER BOTTLE!!

YOU CAN'T BE THIRSTY ALREADY?!! YOU JUST HAD A BREAK A MINUTE AGO.

**Panel 2:** NO! THIS IS TO POUR ON THAT KID WHO TRIED TO TRIP ME.

BRIAN BASSET

**Panel 3:** RORY, PASS THE BALL. ATTA-BOY! NATHAN, LOOK FOR KEEGAN ON YOUR LEFT... GOOD... GOOD... NOW KEEGAN, PASS IT TO TREVOR!...

UM, EXCUSE ME. BUT I NOTICE YOU HAVEN'T BEEN PLAYING MY SON AS MUCH AS SOME OF THE OTHER KIDS.....

**Panel 4:** CLAYTON?? HE'S BEEN IN THE WHOLE GAME.

**Panel 5:** THERE HE IS — ON THE OTHER SIDE OF THE FIELD PLAYING WITH THE DIRT.

**Panel 6:** BRIAN BASSET

NEXT TIME YOU SAY SOMETHING TO THE COACH.

**Panel 7:** I CAN'T BELIEVE COACH PUT ME IN GOAL.

**Panel 8:** OH, NO! AND HERE COMES THE OTHER TEAM WITH THE BALL NOW!

BRIAN BASSET

**Panel 9:** NO FEAR. I CAN'T SHOW THEM ANY FEAR! IN FACT, I NEED TO SHOW THE OPPOSITE!

**Panel 10:** CLAYTON!! MOVE WITH THE BALL! SHIFT! SHIFT! YOUR HANDS!.. YOU CAN USE YOUR HANDS!!

HERE'S TYRANNOSAURUS REX, KING OF THE MEAT EATERS, PROTECTING WHAT IS HIS.

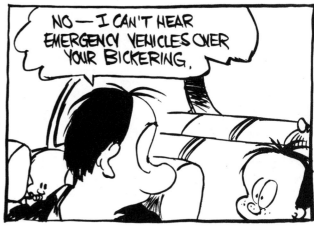

Don't look at it as working alone.  Look at it as having
co-workers you trust and respect.

DADDY. WOULD YOU SIGN THIS CONSENT FORM?.. MY CLASS IS GOING ON A FIELD TRIP TO THE ZOO TOMORROW.

NO PROB!

SCRIBBLE SCRIBBLE SCRIBBLE

THANKS. NOW COULD YOU SIGN MINE?

WHAT DID I JUST SIGN?

YOURS. YOU JUST AGREED TO BE A PARENT/VOLUNTEER AND RIDE THE BUS WITH US ON OUR FIELD TRIP.

BRIAN BASSET

FOR OPTIMUM VISUAL EFFECT; SHAKE PAGE UP AND DOWN WHILE READING.

BRIAN BASSET

DADDY. AREN'T YOU GLAD YOU...

SMASH!

BOUNCE!

...GET TO COME ALONG WITH MY CLASS TO THE ZOO?!

YOU'RE SQUISHING ME, MR. NEWMAN.

ADAM. YOU HAVE JOSH, JOE, AMANDA, TYLER, AND OF COURSE KATY.

YOU CAN TOUR THE ZOO IN ANY ORDER YOU'D LIKE. JUST MAKE SURE YOU HAVE YOUR GROUP AT THE PAVILION BY NOON FOR LUNCH.

BRIAN BASSET

YOU HEARD MRS. NEWBILL. WHAT WOULD YOU LIKE TO SEE FIRST?... THE ELEPHANTS?... THE REPTILES?... WHAT?

THE GIFT SHOP!

**If you've been downsized, try to keep a positive attitude.**

# Ad@m

BY BRIAN BASSET →

SCRIBB SCRIBBLE SCRIBBEE SCRIBB

WHAT D'YA THINK?

TOO SCARY, MIGHT PROMOTE VIOLENCE.

SCRIBBLE SCRIBBLE

OKAY, HOW'S THAT?

NO. COULD BE OFFENSIVE TO CERTAIN ETHNIC GROUPS.

WHAT ABOUT NOW?

TOO GOOFY. THE MENTALLY CHALLENGED MIGHT NOT FIND IT FUNNY.

FINE, WE'LL HAVE A PLAIN, FACELESS JACK-O-LANTERN WITH NOTHING ON IT WHATSOEVER.

JACK??

HOW'S THE CARVING GOING?

POLITICAL CORRECTNESS HAS REARED ITS UGLY HEAD.

DON'T SAY UGLY!! NOT EVERYONE CAN BE BEAUTIFUL, Y'KNOW!

BRIAN BASSET

37

**Another nice thing about working from home:
pilfering the supply cabinet is no longer a crime.**

40

**Panel 1:** ADAM'S BEEN SPENDING SO MUCH TIME ON THE COMPUTER LATELY THAT I'M BEGINNING TO WONDER IF HE ISN'T SEEKING OR DOESN'T ALREADY HAVE A SECRET CYBER-LOVER ON THE INTERNET.

THERE'S ALWAYS A WAY TO FIND OUT.

**Panel 2:** I WAS ONLY JOKING. **HOW?!**

**Panel 3:** USE MY COMPUTER AND SCREEN NAME. E-MAIL HIM A, Y'KNOW, SUGGESTIVE LETTER AND SEE WHAT HIS RESPONSE IS.

**Panel 4:** I COULDN'T.

BRIAN BASSET

BUT YOU'LL BE ME, AND I COULD.

**Panel 5:** YOU HAVE MAIL.

**Panel 6:** DEAR ADAMATHOME. I GOT YOUR ADDRESS FROM THE AT-HOME-DAD NEWSLETTER.

BRIAN BASSET

**Panel 7:** I'M A 32-YEAR-OLD STAY-AT-HOME MOM OF THREE. MY HUSBAND IS *ALWAYS* AWAY. I NEED SOMEONE TO TALK TO.

**Panel 8:** SOMEONE WHO WILL LISTEN TO WHAT GOES ON IN MY DAY. ...AND WHAT *DOESN'T* IN MY NIGHTS.

**Panel 9:** DEAR ADAMATHOME. WHAT'RE YOU WEARING RIGHT NOW? —HOTMAMAWITHKIDS.

**Panel 10:** DON'T YOU THINK THAT'S RATHER PERSONAL?

CLICK CLICK CLICK CLICK CLICK

**Panel 11:** LET ME REPHRASE THAT. HAVE YOU DONE ANY LAUNDRY TODAY?

BRIAN BASSET

**Panel 12:** NO. I'M STILL WEARING THE SAME CLOTHES I HAD ON YESTERDAY.

CLICK CLICK CLICK CLICK

**Panel 13:** THAT'S WHAT I THOUGHT.

42

WHAT'CHA WATCHING?

THIS REALLY COOL NATURE SERIES ON PUBLIC TELEVISION.

THEY'RE SHOWING HOW THE FEMALE PRAYING MANTIS BITES THE HEAD OFF THE MALE PRAYING MANTIS AFTER THEY MAKE BABIES.

BRIAN BASSET

WHAT'S ON THE TUBE?

SEX AND VIOLENCE.

BRIAN BASSET

TRAFFIC WAS AWFUL AGAIN COMING HOME!...AND IT'S ONLY GETTING WORSE!

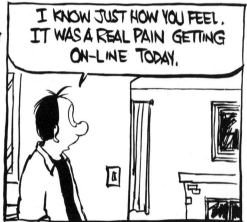

I KNOW JUST HOW YOU FEEL. IT WAS A REAL PAIN GETTING ON-LINE TODAY.

BRIAN BASSET

SHUT!

THUD!

THE PUMPKIN PIES STILL HAVE ANOTHER 5 MINUTES TO BAKE.

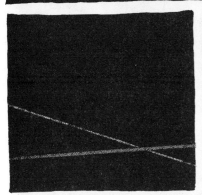

46

No matter how much you may enjoy working from home,
there will always be former co-workers you miss.

DEAR ADAMATHOME. MY HUSBAND IS MARRIED TO HIS WORK, AND FRANKLY, I MIGHT AS WELL NOT EVEN EXIST.

CLICK CLICK CLICK

TO COMPLICATE THINGS— HE'S WORTH MILLIONS. AND I'VE GROWN ACCUSTOMED TO THE LAVISH LIFESTYLE I ENJOY AND DESERVE.

CLICK CLICK CLICK

WHAT SHOULD I DO?

CLICK CLICK

LEAVE HIM. IF WHAT YOU SAY IS TRUE, HE PROBABLY WON'T EVEN NOTICE YOU'RE GONE, AND YOU'LL STILL BE PART OF THE FAMILY FORTUNE.

CLICK CLICK CLICK

HI. HOW'D ADVISING THE WORLD'S HOME OFFICE WORKERS GO TODAY?

I GOT FIRED. GLOBAL ONLINE FIRED ME.

ALL I DID WAS TELL SOME WOMAN TRAPPED IN A PATHETIC RELATIONSHIP TO DUMP THE LOSER.

BUT WASN'T THAT THE REASON FOR HIRING YOU ??... TO GIVE ADVICE?

YEAH... EXCEPT THE "LOSER" TURNED OUT TO BE THE PRESIDENT OF GLOBAL ONLINE.

ADAM. REMEMBER THAT FAMOUS ANTI-SMOKING COMMERCIAL WHEN WE WERE YOUNG..?.....

THE ONE WHERE THIS DAD IS DOING FUN THINGS WITH HIS LITTLE BOY, LIKE TAKING HIM TO THE ZOO AND SUCH — AND THEN THEY SIT AGAINST A TREE AND HE PULLS OUT A PACK OF CIGARETTES...

RIGHT! RIGHT! AND THE LITTLE BOY THINKS HE SHOULD DO THE SAME. AND THEN THIS TV VOICE COMES ON AND SAYS..."LIKE FATHER, LIKE SON."

YOU BET I REMEMBER THAT COMMERCIAL! IT HAD A BIG IMPACT ON ME.

DAVE! HEY, IT'S ADAM. LISTEN— I'M THINKING OF STARTING UP SOMETHING LIKE A BOOK GROUP. INTERESTED?

I WAS HOPING TO GET SOME OF THE OL' SOFTBALL CREW TOGETHER ONCE A MONTH TO DISCUSS THINGS LIKE GREED, PASSION, MONEY, DEBT, POWER, LUST, REDEMPTION, LOST OPPORTUNITIES, ETC.

BRIAN BASSET

BOOKS?? SURE. THOSE TOO.

GUESS WHAT?! I FORMED A BOOK GROUP WITH SOME OF THE GUYS FROM SOFTBALL.

MOM'S HOME! MOM'S HOME!

WE'RE GONNA MEET ONCE A MONTH AT THE SPORTS BAR & GRILL THAT SPONSORED OUR TEAM. OUR FIRST GET-TOGETHER IS THIS MONDAY.

BRIAN BASSET

GEE. A REAL LITERARY HOT SPOT.

I KNOW! THEY EVEN HAVE A SIGNED PAIR OF DENNIS RODMAN'S PANTYHOSE HANGING UP!... AND HE WROTE A BEST SELLER!

... AND AN ORDER OF SUPER-NACHOS.

OKAY! THE FIRST MEETING OF OUR BOOK GROUP IS OFFICIALLY UNDER WAY!

EXPLAIN EXACTLY HOW THIS BOOK GROUP THING WORKS.

WELL... WE PICK A BOOK AS A GROUP, READ IT, DISCUSS IT... AND SHARE OUR FEELINGS.

BRIAN BASSET

THAT'S BACKWARD! WE SHOULD DISCUSS THE BOOK IN DETAIL FIRST. I NEED TO KNOW IF IT'S REALLY WORTH MY TIME AND MONEY.

I DON'T SHARE MY FEELINGS WITH ANYBODY!

GO TO SLEEP UP THERE! IT'S A SCHOOL NIGHT.

ISN'T THERE SOMETHING ELSE ON?.. WHERE'S THE CHANNEL CHANGER?

THERE WERE NUMEROUS B-17 MODIFICATIONS AND CHANGES FOR PERFORMANCE AND COMBAT...

I DUNNO. I THINK ONE OF THE KIDS CARRIED IT OFF.

WELL, I'M NOT WATCHING TV IF I HAVE TO CHANGE THE CHANNELS BY HAND!

OH MY GOSH— THAT'S SOMETHING ADAM WOULD SAY!

PLEASE NO!..NOT MY WORST FEAR OF MARRIAGE!...THAT COUPLES EVENTUALLY DO TAKE ON SIMILAR CHARACTERISTICS AND THE APPEARANCE OF THEIR SPOUSE!!!

LOOK AT THE WAY I'M SITTING ON THE COUCH. I'M SITTING JUST LIKE ADAM!!

I'M EVEN WATCHING A DOCUMENTARY ON WORLD WAR II AIRCRAFT!... JUST LIKE ADAM!!

THE ONLY PROTECTION THE WAIST GUNNERS OF A B-17 HAD WAS...

MAYBE WHAT THEY SAY ABOUT MARRIED COUPLES TAKING ON THE SAME TRAITS AS THEIR SPOUSE IS TRUE!

WHERE ARE YOU GOING?

THE OTHER ROOM TO READ A BOOK. I CAN'T WATCH THIS SHOW ANYMORE.

B-17 FORTRESS AT WAR

DON'T TAKE THIS THE WRONG WAY, ADAM. BUT AS WE GROW OLDER TOGETHER, I DON'T WANT TO BECOME MORE LIKE YOU.

BRIAN BASSET

WHAT ATTRACTED ME TO YOU IN THE FIRST PLACE WAS THE VERY FACT YOU WERE QUITE DIFFERENT FROM ME.

AND THAT YOU'VE CONTINUED TO BRING INTO MY LIFE AND OUR MARRIAGE THAT UNIQUE WAY OF SEEING AND DOING THINGS THE ADAM WAY.

NOW, COULD YOU PLEASE KNOCK IT OFF AND BE-COME MORE LIKE ME?!

**Row 1:**

CLAYTON, DON'T YOU HAVE SOME HOMEWORK TO DO?

NOPE.

YOU HAVE **NO** HOMEWORK YOU COULD BE DOING RIGHT NOW??

NONE.

BRIAN BASSET

MRS. NEWBILL DIDN'T SEND YOU HOME WITH <u>ANY</u> ASSIGNMENTS??

NO, SHE DID.

I LEFT MY BACKPACK ON THE BUS.

**Row 2:**

I'M THINKING OF HOSTING A HOME-OFFICE HOLIDAY PARTY!

WHO WOULD YOU INVITE?

BRIAN BASSET

MY CO-WORKERS, OF COURSE!

YOUR CO-WORKERS??

WELL, YEAH. THERE'S THE GANG AT THE COPY CENTER... THE PEOPLE AT THE OFFICE SUPPLY STORE... THE FED-EX DRIVER WHO PICKS UP AT THE DROP-BOX... THE FOLKS AT MY FAVORITE ESPRESSO PLACE...

NO WONDER YOU'RE NOT AS PRODUCTIVE AROUND HERE AS YOU'D LIKE... YOU'RE <u>NEVER</u> HOME.

**Row 3:**

JUST HOW MANY GUESTS ARE YOU EXPECTING FOR THIS HOME-OFFICE CHRISTMAS PARTY OF YOURS, ADAM?

"HOLIDAY," NOT Christmas.

BRIAN BASSET

THIS IS A SECULAR PARTY.

STRICTLY **PC**, HUH?

NO, THERE'LL BE MACINTOSH PEOPLE AS WELL.

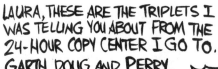

Row 1:
- HAPPY HOLIDAYS, GUYS! COME ON IN! GLAD YOU COULD MAKE IT!
- LAURA, THESE ARE THE TRIPLETS I WAS TELLING YOU ABOUT FROM THE 24-HOUR COPY CENTER I GO TO. GARTH, DOUG AND PERRY.
- I'M IMPRESSED. PERFECT COPIES.
- ACTUALLY, HIS TONES ARE OFF.
- HE'S STILL SORE THAT I WAS COLLATED TWO MINUTES EARLIER.
- I'M PERFECT.

BRIAN BASSET

Row 2:
- HORS D'OEUVRES?
- INTERESTING. WHAT ARE THEY?
- LITTLE BREADS CUT INTO THE SHAPE OF TINY CD-ROMS AND PUT UNDER THE BROILER WITH CHEESE ON 'EM.
- OH. OKAY.
- WHY, YOU EVEN PUT ITSY-BITSY SMUDGES ALL OVER THEM TO MAKE 'EM LOOK LIKE THEY'VE BEEN HANDLED BY REAL KIDS.
- THAT'S BECAUSE THEY HAVE BEEN HANDLED BY REAL KIDS.
- OH, GOODY— HORS D'OEUVRES!

BRIAN BASSET

Row 3:
- WHAT A MESS. I THOUGHT THEY'D NEVER LEAVE.
- KNOCK KNOCK~
- WE'RE BACK!!
- NONE OF US CAN GET OUT YOUR STREET, IT'S SNOWING SO HARD!

BRIAN BASSET

**No home office is complete without a fax machine.**

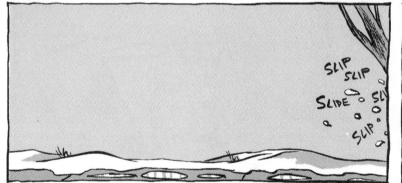

64

WHAT'RE WE GOING TO DO, ADAM??

WITHOUT MY INCOME WE CAN'T AFFORD THIS HOUSE... OUR CARS... OR EVEN MEDICAL INSURANCE.

WE JUST WON'T GET SICK OR INJURED.

TRY TELLING THAT TO A HOUSE FULL OF RAMBUNCTIOUS KIDS AND A BABY.

PUT DOWN THAT CHRISTMAS CARD!! YOU MIGHT GET A PAPER CUT!

LOOK! IT'S SNOWING! EVEN WITH YOU LOSING YOUR JOB THIS WEEK, LAURA, THERE'S STILL BEAUTY TO BE FOUND.

BEAUTY?? ALL I CAN SEE ARE THE FIVE OF US HOMELESS AND OUT IN THE COLD.

UM... LET'S SIT BY THE FIRE INSTEAD.

NOW ALL I SEE ARE OUR LIFE'S SAVINGS GOING UP IN SMOKE. ...BURNING AWAY....

ADAM, UNTIL I'M ABLE TO FIND A JOB, WE ARE GOING TO HAVE TO WATCH EVERY PENNY WE SPEND.

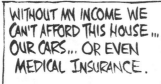

THAT MEANS YOU NEED TO CUT BACK ON YOUR LATTES, OR DOUBLE-TALL MOCHAS OR WHATEVER IT IS YOU GO OUT FOR.

WHAT??!? I'D RATHER PAINT MYSELF BLUE AND RUN AROUND TOWN NAKED BEFORE I DID THAT!

HMMMMMM... WITH THE MONEY WE'D SAVE ON CLOTHES....

IT'S ALMOST 10 A.M. AREN'T YOU PLANNING ON BEING PRODUCTIVE?

I'M DRESSED.

BRIAN BASSET

AT WORK, WE WOULD'VE ALREADY FIRED OFF A DOZEN MEMOS AND ATTENDED HALF THAT MANY MEETINGS BY 10 O'CLOCK.

AND YOU CALL ME UNPRODUCTIVE??

OH MY GOSH—DID YOU SEE THAT?!!? NICK JUST PULLED HIMSELF UP AND WALKED!!

BRIAN BASSET

AND DID YOU HEAR WHAT HE JUST SAID?? HE SAID, "LUB MAMA." HE SAID HE LOVES HIS MAMA!!!

AND THIS MORNING!!..THIS MORNING I SAW HIM EAT SOLID FOODS!!

WHILE AT THE OFFICE, I GUESS YOU MISSED MORE OF HIS GROWING UP THAN I THOUGHT.

NOW HE'S SUCKING HIS THUMB!! HE'S SUCKING HIS THUMB JUST LIKE A REAL BABY!!!

I'VE GOTTA GET THE VIDEO CAMERA. ...DON'T WANT TO MISS ANY OF YOUR REACTIONS.

I'M GONNA TAKE NICK FOR A STROLL. WANNA COME WITH US?

NO. YOU GO WITHOUT ME. I HAVE A LOT OF E-MAIL TO ANSWER.

I ALWAYS IMAGINED HOW NICE IT WOULD BE TO TAKE LONG WALKS WITH YOU AND NICK IF I EVER FOUND MYSELF HOME DURING THE WEEK......AND NOW THAT I'M SUDDENLY UNEMPLOYED...

OKAY, OKAY, I'LL GO!

ADAM, YOU'RE DAWDLING.

THE EXTENSION CORD TO THE COMPUTER WON'T REACH ANY FARTHER.

BRIAN BASSET

ADAM

BY BRIAN BASSET

EXCUSE ME.

WHAT HAPPENED TO THE LITTLE NEIGHBORHOOD VIDEO STORE THAT USED TO BE HERE?

WE BOUGHT THEM OUT THURSDAY, BULLDOZED IT FRIDAY, AND BUILT THIS MEGASTORE ON SATURDAY.

ALL THIS IN ONLY THREE DAYS?!?

WE MOVE FAST TO SERVE THE VIDEO-RENTING PUBLIC BETTER.

NOW THEN, HOW MAY I HELP YOU?

OH, RIGHT. UM... DO YOU HAVE ANY COPIES OF 'CASABLANCA'?

BRIAN BASSET

CASA...... CASA......

IT STARS HUMPHREY BOGART.

BOGART?? BOGART??

YEAH. HE PLAYED TOUGH GUYS.

OH, LIKE A STALLONE, OR SCHWARZENEGGER!? WE STOCK OVER 75,000 COPIES OF THEIR MOVIES IN THIS STORE ALONE!

NOPE. NO CASA-WHATEVER. YOU MIGHT WANT TO TRY ONE OF THOSE LITTLE NEIGHBORHOOD VIDEO STORES FOR THAT.

One way to ensure productivity while kids are also home
is to invest in a laptop.

SERIOUSLY, IT'S NO TROUBLE TO REARRANGE MY SCHEDULE... I'M JUST SO PLEASED YOU HAVE TIME FOR ME!!....UH-HUH....UH-HUN.... GREAT! SEE YOU THEN!! OH, AND THANK YOU THANK YOU THANK YOU THANK YOU THANK YOU THANK YOU!!

GEEESH. I HEARD ALL THAT. YOU DON'T THINK YOU CAME ACROSS AS A BIT TOO ANXIOUS FOR THE JOB?

JOB??

NO, THAT WAS MY HAIRDRESSER. THE JOB INTERVIEWS I HAVE AREN'T UNTIL LATER IN THE WEEK.

BRIAN BASSET

WELL, IT WAS STILL PATHETIC THE WAY YOU SUCKED UP TO HIM.

HEY. THIS IS A MAN WITH THE POWER TO MAKE MY HAIR LOOK LIKE A BADLY MOWED LAWN AND ABOUT THE SAME COLOR, TOO.

AN ALL-DAY FIELD TRIP WITH KATY'S CLASS?!? YOU COMMITTED ME TO GO ON AN ALL-DAY FIELD TRIP?!!

YES. I SHOULD'VE ASKED YOU, BUT I GUESS I DIDN'T THINK YOU'D MIND SO MUCH.

FINE! WHATEVER! I'LL DO IT. I KNOW YOU GO ON A LOT OF THESE THINGS.

IT'S JUST THAT I HAVE JOB INTERVIEWS LATER THIS WEEK TO PREPARE FOR.

I'D GO MYSELF, BUT I MIGHT HAVE A MEETING WITH A SMALL-BUSINESS REP FROM THE, UM, PHONE COMPANY.

BRIAN BASSET

OH. AND DID I TELL YOU YOU WERE DRIVING?!

DADDY, WE'RE HOME!

DID YOU HAVE A FUN TIME ON YOUR FIELD TRIP?

UH-HUH! WE LEARNED ALL ABOUT TIRES AND SIDEWALLS!...AND THE NICE MAN AT THE SERVICE STATION SHOWED US WHEN A TIRE CAN AND CAN'T BE REPAIRED!... AND WE ALSO EARNED SOME MONEY TOO!!

TIRES?? MONEY?? I THOUGHT YOU WERE GOING TO THE AQUARIUM?

LAST @★!!%! FIELD TRIP I DRIVE!

AW'RIGHT! ANOTHER 25¢ FOR A BAD WORD!

BRIAN BASSET

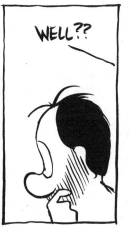

**Ad@m**

By Brian Basset

SIGH...

I NEED TO GET A JOB FIRST JUST TO AFFORD SOME DECENT CLOTHES TO WEAR TO A JOB INTERVIEW.

I HAVE A BIG JOB INTERVIEW TOMORROW, ADAM. WANNA HELP?

LIKE IN ROLE-PLAYING? SURE!

GREAT! OKAY... ASK ME SOMETHING ABOUT MY BACKGROUND.

UM... WHERE WERE YOU PREVIOUSLY EMPLOYED AND FOR HOW LONG?

WELL... FOR THE PAST 12 YEARS I WORKED AT...

**YOU'RE HIRED**

SERIOUSLY, ADAM! HELP ME OUT HERE.

FOR THE PAST 12 YEARS I WORKED AT...

**YOU'RE HIRED**

ARRRGG—YOU'RE NO HELP! YOU'RE **TOO** BIASED!

STOMP STOMP STOMP

NO. JUST TIRED OF EATING AT HOME.

BRIAN BASSET

THOSE WHO'VE NEVER WORKED FROM THEIR HOME THINK THOSE OF US WHO DO HAVE IT SO EASY. WHAT THEY FAIL TO TAKE INTO ACCOUNT ARE ALL THE DISTRACTIONS. LIKE TODAY, I COULD HARDLY CONCENTRATE.

BRIAN BASSET

WHAT DISTRACTIONS?? CLAYTON AND KATY DIDN'T GET HOME FROM SCHOOL UNTIL AFTER 3, AND I WAS OUT AND ABOUT WITH NICK ALL DAY.

WELL... THERE'S THE REFRIGERATOR... THE PANTRY... THE TV... THE VCR......

I NEVER HAD TO DEAL WITH ANY OF THOSE WHEN I WORKED IN AN OFFICE.

BOY, I HOPE ROSIE DOESN'T HAVE AN INTERESTING SHOW TOMORROW.

PLEASE LORD, TELL ME OUR CHILDREN DIDN'T GET HIS WEIRDNESS GENES!

I'LL HAVE A TRIPLE-TALL NONFAT MOCHA WITH LOTS OF FOAM AND NO WHIPPED CREAM FOR HERE!

SEE, ANNIE! THAT'S WHAT I LIKE IN A MAN. DECISIVENESS!

BRIAN BASSET

ONLY... MAYBE MAKE HIM FOUR INCHES TALLER... 10 YEARS YOUNGER... AND GIVE HIM A FULL HEAD OF HAIR.

ON SECOND THOUGHT, MAKE THAT TO GO.

I DON'T GET IT. ALL THIS FOOD AND HE'S STILL BEGGING.

JUST GIVE HIM SOME QUARTERS SO WE CAN EAT IN PEACE.

I SAID NO MORE! OH, OKAY...

BRIAN BASSET

I'D LIKE TO BUY THIS BOOK. "HOW TO GET THE PERFECT JOB."

Y'KNOW, YOU MIGHT WANNA CONSIDER HOLDING OFF ON THIS PURCHASE FOR A BIT. THEY'RE HIRING HERE IF YOU'RE INTERESTED.

IS IT THE PERFECT JOB?

HEAVENS NO!

BUT THEN YOU'LL AT LEAST GET A 30 PERCENT EMPLOYEE DISCOUNT.

BRIAN BASSET

---

THEY SAID THAT YOU WERE THE ONE TO SEE ABOUT THE JOB OPENING.

THAT'S RIGHT. I'M TONYA, THE ASSISTANT MANAGER.

THE POSITION IS FOR A BOOKSELLER, ALTHOUGH IT WOULD BE NICE TO HAVE SOMEONE OF YOUR GENERATION HELPING WITH THE CLASSICAL MUSIC SECTION.

BRIAN BASSET

GEE, GUESS I'M YOUR GIRL THEN... SEEING HOW I STILL HAVE AN OLD ALBUM WITH "ROLL OVER BEETHOVEN" ON IT AT HOME.

PERFECT! I'VE EVEN HEARD OF HIM.

UM... WHAT'S AN ALBUM, THOUGH?

---

IF THEY OFFER YOU THE JOB AT THE BOOKSTORE, I THINK YOU SHOULD TAKE IT.

REALLY?? IT DOESN'T PAY THAT MUCH.

YEAH... BUT IT HAS MEDICAL AND DENTAL BENEFITS..... IT'S CLOSE TO HOME.....

AND IT HAS A CAFE WHERE I CAN GET ESPRESSO DRINKS AT HALF PRICE WITH YOUR EMPLOYEE DISCOUNT!

BRIAN BASSET

GOOD POINT! THAT LAST ONE COULD SAVE US A FEW THOUSAND DOLLARS A YEAR.

WE'RE HOME!

I WONDER WHERE MOM IS.

DAD, WHERE'S MOM? SHE USUALLY GREETS US AT THE DOOR.

BRIAN BASSET

MOM WENT BACK TO WORK, REMEMBER?

RIGHT.

I WAS WONDERING IF I COULD TAKE A BREAK AND RUN HOME TO GREET MY KIDS AT THE DOOR?!

RIGHT!!! HERE, SHELVE THESE BOOKS.

Y'KNOW, IT WAS NICE HAVING MY WIFE AROUND THE HOUSE THE LAST FEW MONTHS. BUT TO BE HONEST, I'M KINDA GLAD SHE'S GONE BACK TO WORK.

BRIAN BASSET

TAKE MY LATE-MORNING NAPS, FOR INSTANCE. I COULD NEVER GET HER TO SEE THAT THEY WERE THE **TIME** EQUIVALENT OF THE COFFEE BREAKS I USED TO TAKE WHEN I WORKED AT AN OFFICE.

MAKES PERFECT SENSE TO ME. I CAN SEE WHY YOU'RE UNEMPLOYED. DO I KNOW YOU??

EMILY, WANNA PLAY SOMETHING OTHER THAN "TEATIME"?

SURE, LIKE WHAT?

I DUNNO... HOW'BOUT SOMETHING LIKE **SPACE SHUTTLE**? WE COULD PRETEND TO BE UP IN SPACE AND HAVE TO FIX A BROKEN SATELLITE.

BRIAN BASSET

AND THEN SOMETHING GOES TERRIBLY WRONG AND ONE OF OUR FELLOW ASTRONAUTS ENDS UP FLOATING HELPLESSLY THROUGH SPACE FOR EVER AND EVER WHEN HIS LIFE-LINE MYSTERIOUSLY SNAPS.

OKAY!

CLAYTON, WANNA PLAY WITH US?

# Ad@m

By Brian Basset

I DUNNO, ADAM. I'M STARTING TO THINK YOU HAVE SOMETHING KINKY GOING ON WITH THAT COMPUTER.

AND HOW'S THAT?

WELL... LOOK AT YOU! YOU'RE JUST SITTING THERE AND IT'S NOT EVEN TURNED ON.

DO I NOT TURN YOU ON?

ALWAYS!! YOU KNOW I CAN'T RESIST THE STUBBLE LOOK!

**If you run a home-based business, keep good records.**

**Of course, it helps to find an accountant
who works from his home as well.**

EXCUSE ME. I'M INTERESTED IN BUYING THIS BOOK BUT WAS WONDERING IF I COULD GET AN ADDITIONAL DISCOUNT ON IT?

WHILE THUMBING THROUGH IT I COULDN'T HELP BUT NOTICE THE COFFEE STAINS ON THE PAGES.

BRIAN BASSET

WELL, DUHHH, LADY! YOU'RE DRINKING A LATTE IN THE STORE! DID IT EVER OCCUR TO YOU THAT YOU'RE A SLOB?!?

NO. BUT I'D BE HAPPY TO ORDER YOU A NEW COPY.

NICK. THIS IS CLARA. CLARA'S GONNA BE WITH US FOR A FEW HOURS WHILE HER MOMMY RUNS SOME ERRANDS. SO PLAY NICELY.

BRIAN BASSET

AND SHARE.

HOW WAS SCHOOL TODAY?

IT WAS GREAT!

Y'KNOW TREVOR IN MY CLASS? WELL, TODAY'S HIS BIRTHDAY. AND ON YOUR BIRTHDAY, MRS. NEWBILL LETS YOU RUN THE CLASS FOR THE LAST 15 MINUTES BEFORE THE BELL RINGS.

BRIAN BASSET

AND DID HE?

HE SURE DID!

UP AND DOWN THE HALLS THROUGH THE LIBRARY AND INTO THE MULTIPURPOSE ROOM, PAST THE OFFICE, OUTSIDE AND AROUND THE SCHOOL THREE TIMES.

WHO IS BETH?

SHE'S, UM... Y'KNOW, UM... A MOM I'VE BEEN CHATTING WITH ONLINE.

THAT'S NICE.

YOU'RE NOT JEALOUS??

HEAVENS NO. I'M GLAD YOU'VE FOUND SOMEONE OTHER THAN ME TO GRIPE TO ABOUT SPIT-UP STAINS, DIAPERS, MAKING LUNCHES, CAR POOLS AND WHATEVER ELSE.

BRIAN BASSET

I TAKE THAT BACK. MY WIFE DOES UNDERSTAND ME.

CLICK CLICK CLICK CLICK CLICK CLICK CLICK

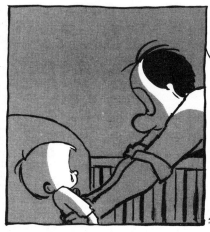

MY GOODNESS. YOU'RE SOAKING.

I SUPPOSE ALL THAT DROOL HAS TO GO SOMEWHERE WHEN YOU'RE ASLEEP.

BRIAN BASSET

ADAM, WHAT'RE YOU DOING HERE? DIDN'T YOU GET MY MESSAGE??

I E-MAILED EVERYONE AND SAID I HAD TO CANCEL MOTHER/BABY GROUP AT MY HOUSE TODAY. ERIN'S SICK.

OH, YEAH. I GUESS I DID.

BRIAN BASSET

UM... GOT ANY BANANA BREAD OR COFFEE CAKE I COULD TAKE WITH ME?

**RING**

MR. NEWMAN'S OFFICE. MR. NEWMAN STEPPED AWAY FOR A MOMENT. MAY I TAKE A MESSAGE?

UH-HUH... UH-HUH... I'LL LET HIM KNOW YOU PHONED, BYE.

BRIAN BASSET

MR. NEWMAN, YOU'RE BACK. AMERICAN EXPRESS CALLED,

THE USUAL? A DOUBLE-TALL, NONFAT MOCHA FOR HERE, RIGHT?

RIGHT! FOR HERE.

BRIAN BASSET

EXCUSE ME, MISS. BUT THERE'S THIS BOOK.

OKAY....

NEW RELEASES

WELL, I CAN'T REMEMBER THE TITLE OR THE AUTHOR, OR EVEN THE FULL SUBJECT. BUT THEY WERE TALKING ABOUT IT ON THE RADIO AND IT SOUNDED GOOD,

MAYBE YOU SHOULD CALL THE RADIO STATION AND ASK THEM.

BRIAN BASSET

I DON'T REMEMBER WHICH STATION IT WAS. DO YOU KNOW THE ONE?!

**The fewer promises you make the more you'll keep.**

**Think big. It's not uncommon for the head of a major corporation to have a TV, VCR, and sofa in their conference room.**

# Ad@m

## BY BRIAN BASSET

A WEB SITE!!

SAY WHAT??

A WEB SITE! IF I HAD MY OWN WEB SITE, I'D PROBABLY INCREASE SALES TENFOLD!

BRIAN BASSET

HOW MUCH WILL THIS WEB SITE COST US, ADAM?

WHO KNOWS. BUT YA GOTTA SPEND MONEY TO MAKE MONEY.

PROBABLY FIRST SAID BY A COUNTERFEITER TO HIS WIFE AS HE WAS TRYING TO EXPLAIN THE NEW PRINTING PRESS IN THEIR BASEMENT.

YEAH, WELL... ONLY 'CAUSE HIS WIFE DIDN'T HAVE ANY FAITH IN HIM.

I'LL GIVE YOU A BACKRUB IF YOU RETURN THE VIDEO BEFORE MIDNIGHT.

NOPE.

OKAY. A BACKRUB AND A FOOT MASSAGE!?

I'D RATHER PAY THE LATE CHARGE.

BRIAN BASSET

I REMEMBER WHEN YOU USED TO DO ANYTHING I ASKED OF YOU, ADAM.

LIKE WHEN WE WERE FIRST MARRIED?

YEAH.

WE DIDN'T OWN A VCR BACK THEN.

HAVE YOU DECIDED YET IF YOU'RE PLAYING BASEBALL THIS YEAR? I NEED TO KNOW. FORMS ARE DUE BACK NEXT WEEK.

IS IT COACH-PITCH LIKE LAST YEAR?

LOOK. I TOLD YOU— I WAS PRESSED INTO SERVICE. I CAN'T BELIEVE YOU'RE STILL SORE AT ME FOR HITTING YOU WITH THE PITCH.

BRIAN BASSET

NO, I'M NOT SORE ANYMORE. ALTHOUGH I STILL GET DIZZY SPELLS.

YOU MEAN YOU'RE *NOT* MARTHA STEWART?!?

THAT'S WHAT I'VE BEEN TRYING TO TELL YOU.

I'M HER THIRD COUSIN TWICE REMOVED, MARLA. I'M A WEB PAGE DESIGNER. YOU E-MAILED MY COMPANY THAT YOU WANTED A WEB SITE FOR YOUR BUSINESS.

TWICE REMOVED??

YES, FROM MARTHA'S SUMMER HOME ON THE HAMPTONS, I DARED TO BE CRITICAL OF CHINTZ.

BRIAN BASSET

I CAN'T GET OVER THIS! MARTHA STEWART'S COUSIN IS GONNA DESIGN MY WEB PAGE!! HOW'D YOU GET INTO WEB PAGE DESIGN IN THE FIRST PLACE? UM, MORE COFFEE, MS. STEWART?

NO THANKS.

WELL, I KNEW THAT'S WHERE THE BIG BUCKS WOULD BE!... *NOT* IN SCOURING GARAGE SALES LOOKING FOR DEPRESSION-ERA DINNERWARE OR IN GOLD-LEAFING GARDEN TOOLS.

BRIAN BASSET

YOU DON'T THINK I MADE A BAD CAREER MOVE, DO YOU?

*NOOOOOO*, DON'T BE SILLY!... THAT DEPRESSION-ERA STUFF CAN BE SO... UM... *DEPRESSING*.

EXACTLY!

WHAT DO YOU THINK OF THIS COLOR FOR YOUR BACKGROUND?

I LIKE IT.

BRIAN BASSET

YOU ARE OBVIOUSLY VERY GOOD AT WHAT YOU DO. SO, HAS BEING MARTHA STEWART'S COUSIN BEEN A HINDRANCE OR A HELP?

SUCH AS?

OPENING DOORS— THAT SORT OF THING. I MEAN, THE RESEMBLANCE IS UNCANNY!

YES, IT'S OPENED MANY DOORS. YOU CAN'T BELIEVE HOW DIFFICULT IT IS TO FIND THE RIGHT ADDRESS THROUGH THIS HAIR.

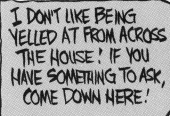

If isolation becomes a factor when working from home . . .

Form a support group. Invite other
at-home-office types over.

LAURA, SEE THAT GENTLEMAN SITTING OVER THERE BY THE WINDOW READING?

HE COMES IN HERE EVERY DAY, TAKES OVER ONE OF OUR CHOICE OVERSTUFFED CHAIRS FOR HOURS LOOKING AT BOOKS, BUT NEVER _EVER_ BUYS ONE.

BRIAN BASSET

DON'T YOU JUST HATE THAT?

ON THE CONTRARY, HE'S OUR **BEST** CUSTOMER! WE GO TO HIM FOR BOOK RECOMMENDATIONS.

STOP!! WHAT DO YOU TWO THINK YOU'RE DOING?!? YOU'RE TRACKING DIRT AND MUD INTO THE HOUSE!

BRIAN BASSET

RIGHT. TODAY'S EARTH DAY.

EXCUSE ME, SIR. BUT ARE THOSE TWO LITTLE CHILDREN — THE ONES TOTALLY UNSUPERVISED AND FLINGING BOOKS OFF THE SHELVES — _YOURS_?!

MAGAZINES

YUP, THEY'RE MINE. BUT THEY'RE **NOT** UNSUPERVISED. **YOU'VE** OBVIOUSLY BEEN WATCHING THEM.

FLIP FLIP FLIP

BRIAN BASSET

WHY AREN'T YOU TWO DRESSED AND READY FOR SCHOOL YET??

TODAY IS "TAKE YOUR CHILD TO WORK" DAY.

I DON'T THINK SO.

NO, IT IS. REALLY.

RATS.

I'M THINKING OF EXPANDING MY BUSINESS...OF OFFERING A LINE OF GREETING CARDS PEOPLE CAN ORDER THROUGH THEIR COMPUTER.

SOUNDS GREAT, ADAM. BUT DON'T THE BIG CARD COMPANIES ALREADY DO THAT?

AND THEIR CARDS COME ACROSS AS BIG AND IMPERSONAL, WHEREAS MY CARDS WILL APPEAR HONEST AND HOMEMADE.

"BELIEVABLE EXCUSES," HUH?

RIGHT! THAT, AND I CAN'T DRAW TO SAVE MY LIFE.

LEMME SEE IF I UNDERSTAND YOU. YOU'RE GOING TO OFFER A LINE OF CARDS THAT'RE INTENDED TO ARRIVE LATE...APPEAR HAND-MADE...AND WHICH WILL CONTAIN SOME SAPPY EXCUSE.

"BELIEVABLE EXCUSE," LAURA. WHY, THERE ARE MILLIONS OF GUYS OUT THERE JUST LIKE ME!

AND WHO BETTER TO OFFER THIS THAN THE MASTER HIMSELF?!

AND YOU THINK FORGETTING OUR ANNIVERSARY BECAUSE YOU WERE SUPPOSEDLY ABDUCTED BY ALIENS WAS A "BELIEVABLE" EXCUSE?!?

I TOLD YOU. I HAVE ABSOLUTELY NO RECOLLECTION OF IT. THEY MUST'VE ERASED MY MEMORY.

OKAY. THAT WOULD EXPLAIN A LOT OF THINGS.

FLIP
FLIP
FLIP
FLIP

**Shopping for office supplies is easy these days.**

I DON'T KNOW WHAT I'M GONNA DO WHEN THEY'RE OUT OF SCHOOL FOR THE SUMMER... THEY'RE ALREADY DRIVING ME CRAZY!

HAVE YOU GIVEN ANY THOUGHT TO SUMMER CAMP?

DO YOU HAVE ANY IDEA HOW EXPENSIVE IT WOULD BE TO SEND THEM?

NOT THEM. **YOU**.

DAAAD!

DING DONG

KEEP RINGING, I'LL SNEAK A PEEK AROUND BACK.

DING DONG DING DONG DING DONG

OPEN UP, ADAM! WE KNOW YOU'RE IN THERE! IT'S YOUR TURN TO HOST THE MOTHER/BABY GROUP FOR COFFEE!

YUP! I SEE HIM IN THE LAUNDRY ROOM GLUED TO HIS COMPUTER.

IN CYBERSPACE— NO ONE CAN HEAR YOU SCREAM.

POUND POUND POUND

DADDY, CAN CARMEN SPEND THE NIGHT?!!

IT'S OKAY WITH ME IF IT'S OKAY WITH HER FOLKS.

C'MON! LET'S CALL!!

YEA!!! THEY SAID I CAN STAY!

HERE'S THE "OBNOXIOUS" NIGHT COMMANDO PUTTING ON HIS MAKEUP....

**Negotiating traffic on the road to *the* information super-highway.**

THE SWIM TEAM?!!? I DON'T WANT TO BE ON THE SWIM TEAM!

THEY PRACTICE TOO EARLY AND THE WATER'S COLD!!

BRIAN BASSET

CLAYTON, WE'VE ALREADY GONE OVER THIS, YOU'RE A GOOD SWIMMER!

YEAH, WELL... FLIPPER'S A GOOD SWIMMER, BUT YOU DON'T FIND DOLPHINS IN COLD WATER!

WELCOME TO SWIM TEAM PRACTICE. MY NAME IS COACH HANNULA.

IT'S C-C-C-C-COLD. I'M MISSING MY MORNING C-C-CARTOONS.

FIRST OFF, I'D LIKE TO BREAK UP INTO GROUPS.

YOU'RE NEVER GETTING ME IN THAT W-W-W-W-WATER.

THOSE IN THE BACK WILL BE IN THE SHARKS.

BRIAN BASSET

THE TWO IN THE FRONT WILL BE BAIT.

THAT'S GOOD! WE'LL GET TO GO HOME SOONER.

CLAYTON! IN THE POOL!!

CHATTER CHATTER CHATTER CHATTER

NO, I'LL DROWN!!

CHATTER CHATTER CHATTER CHATTER CHATTER CHATTER

BRIAN BASSET

AND HOW'S THAT?... SAYS HERE YOU'RE A VERY GOOD SWIMMER.

THE WATER'S TOO COLD AND I CAN'T SWIM WITH MY ARMS CROSSED.

CHATTER CHATTER CHATTER CHATTER CHATTER CHATTER CHATTER

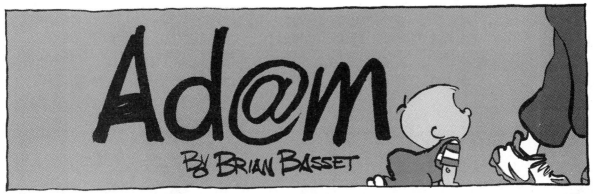

The EVOLUTION of MAN

WELCOME TO YOUR FIRST DAY OF COMPUTER CAMP. MY NAME IS WILLY, AND I'LL BE YOUR CAMP COUNSELOR.

YOU'RE HERE TO SHARPEN YOUR COMPUTER SKILLS AND TO HAVE FUN!!!

TODAY, YOU'LL LEARN HOW EASY IT IS TO ACCESS THE NUCLEAR DEFENSE SYSTEM OF FRANCE.

JUST KIDDING!... THAT'LL BE COVERED IN THE THIRD WEEK.

CONSIDER YOURSELF FORTUNATE, CLAYTON. WHEN I WAS A KID — YOUR GRANDFATHER USED TO BARBECUE THE OLD-FASHIONED WAY.

YOU MEAN WITH CHARCOAL BRIQUETTES?

NOPE. BY POURING LIGHTER FLUID DIRECTLY ONTO THE FOOD.

YOU SAID YOU'D TOSS THE BALL WITH ME, DAD.

AND I WILL, JUST AS SOON AS I'M DONE HERE.

OKAY, TELL YOU WHAT. YOU GO OUTSIDE AND I'LL GRAB MY MITT.

**Working from home is gaining greater acceptance every day.**

**THE END**